LETTER

TO THE

HON. WM. C. RIVES,

OF VIRGINIA,

ON

Slavery and the Union,

BY

NATHAN APPLETON,

OF BOSTON, MASS.

BOSTON:
1860.
J. H. EASTBURN'S PRESS.

LETTER

TO THE

HON. WM. C. RIVES,

OF VIRGINIA,

ON

Slavery and the Union,

BY

NATHAN APPLETON,

OF BOSTON, MASS.

BOSTON:
1860.
J. H. EASTBURN'S PRESS.

LETTER.

My Dear Sir,—

I have read with great satisfaction your letter published in the Richmond Whig, on "The Present Crisis and the Value of the Union." Agreeing with you that it is the duty of every good citizen, so far as may lay in his power, to allay the existing excitement, and to endeavor to bring us back to that state of fraternal feeling under which the North and the South mutually shed their blood to bring this nation into existence, and which for so many years harmonized in its unparalleled prosperity, I address this letter to you, and through you, to the public.

I have, for many years, been retired from an active participation in public affairs, but have not been unobservant of the course of events; and, drawing to the close of a long life, can have no motive but to leave to my children the blessings of a free and stable government, which I have myself so long enjoyed. The present is a period of alarm and excitement greater than we have heretofore witnessed. The North and the South appear in all but hostile array against each other, and all growing out of the subject of Slavery.

A short review of the causes which have led to this state of things will not be out of place, and will, I think, show that there have been faults on both sides.

The first aggression was made by the North, or rather by a few individuals residing in the North. About the year 1830, a very few persons, under the lead of William Lloyd Garrison and Wendell Phillips, formed themselves into an Abolition Society, denouncing and repudiating the Constitution of the United States, in as much as it recognized the existence of Slavery. At home this movement excited little attention: the few individuals comprised in it were considered unfortunate fanatical monomaniacs—rather the objects of pity, than of any other feeling. But they published inflammatory pamphlets, which were sent into the South evidently with the intention of acting upon the slaves. This naturally excited the indignation of the South, but it was difficult to point out any remedy. So absolutely free are we in speech and in the press, that we leave false opinions to be refuted by true ones. But this did not meet the evils of the present case. The South had no course but to take the remedy into their own hands; they took measures to prevent the circulation of their tracts, but not without much irritation.

In 1840, the slaves in the British West Indies were made free, with a compensation to the planters, of twenty millions sterling. This event excited a strong desire amongst a certain class of philanthropists, that we should do the same thing; except, indeed, in the compensation, which I believe was never mentioned. In this movement a number of the clergy took an active part, especially stimulated to do this by a portion of the clergy in England, mostly amongst the dissenters, who proclaimed Slavery to be a sin against God. The more sober part of the community were of the opinion that Slavery is a political institution, and not within the province of the clergy in their character of teachers of religion. As it does not exist amongst us, it was regretted that instead of reforming our own lives, they should be discussing the sins of distant communities. Sin is a matter which rests between the individual and his Maker, and in doubtful cases like this had better be left there. Who constituted weak fallible man the judge and avenger of wrongs done to the infinite Creator? We of the North consider Slavery a social evil; but I think the regret has been general, that the subject has been so mingled with religion. Slavery has been denounced as an evil which must be abated at all events, but no one has undertaken to show how it can be done. Nor can he. Omnipotence alone can do it. Man cannot. The example of England, in the emancipation of her Colonies, has no bearing on the question with us. There is no resemblance in the two cases which makes it practicable, or even possible, in most of our Slave States.

The next important movement took place on the part of the South, in 1848. Up to this period it was held that Slavery was an institution of the individual

States, with which Congress had nothing to do. But it was now discovered that the Constitution gives to the slave a character as property which was never before dreamed of. The first practical demonstration took place on the meeting of Congress in December 1849, when six of the Southern Whigs defeated the election of Mr. Winthrop, as Speaker. I cannot put my own view of the matter in a stronger light than is contained in the following extracts from a letter which I wrote on the 22d December, 1849, to my friend, the Hon. Mr. H———, of Alabama, one of the six, in reply to one from him explanatory of his course.

"I regretted Mr. Toombs introducing his Resolutions into the Whig Caucus, as ill-timed, and to a certain extent, improper. * * * I am under deep apprehension about this Southern excitement, and I am as much surprised as alarmed at its existence. I read Mr. Berrien's Speech in the Senate in 1848, advocating the right to hold slaves in the new Territories, under the Constitution of the United States, with attention and regret. He argued the matter with great ingenuity and ability, but I could not possibly adopt his conclusions. The whole argument appeared to me a rare example of legal subtlety opposed to plain common-sense. This claim of legal right is now further enforced by the additional discovery, that Southern honor is involved in the right to establish Slavery as a personal matter, affecting personal rights and personal honor in regard to every individual residing in the Slave States. Such an appeal excites the most powerful feelings and passions of our nature, and under their influence, in an individual or a community, the most unhappy consequences may be apprehended.

"As a practical question, there seems to be nothing of any importance to quarrel about. There seems to be no part of the new territory suited to the productions on which alone slaves can be profitably employed. In their present condition, there is no law by which the master can hold his slave. It would seem too hazardous an adventure to carry slaves into a region where they could walk off without remedy, except by Lynch law, which would probably take their side. No one can suppose that Congress will ever pass a law establishing Slavery where it does not exist; and yet, I do not see but what the claim of the South to the right to enjoy the new conquests with their slaves, would make it as imperative on Congress to protect them in this right, as it is objectionable for Congress to prohibit Slavery in them. With every disposition to protect the rights of the South as secured by the Constitution, I cannot bring my mind to the Southern view of the right or the honor involved in the case. Suppose Slavery prohibited in all the new Territories,—the prohibition extends to all citizens of the United States. Northern men go into the South and hold slaves. Southern men move into the Free States. There seems nothing in the fact of a man being born or living in a certain latitude, which makes a slave a natural or necessary appendage to him, or which gives him rights not belonging to one born further north, any further than the local law extends. The South claims the right to carry slaves into the Territories, under the general right of every citizen to carry his property. The North objects to slaves, because they are persons, only held as property by a tenure unknown in respect to all other property, the law of force. All our institutions and rights, with this exception, rest on consent—mutual agreement. Slavery is either an evil or a good. Supposing it to be an evil, the natives of the South will escape it and be benefited by removing into Territories where it is prohibited. Supposing Slavery to be a good, the citizen of the North is injured by the prohibition, as well as the citizen of the South. Opinions on this matter may vary with the latitude, but the principle is the same. The Wilmot Proviso appears to me little but an abstraction, a bugbear, a nonentity, wholly unworthy to excite the North or the South to threats of disunion. It affects to prevent what without it cannot by any possibility be done, but which may nevertheless be done whenever the new States choose, the Proviso notwithstanding.

"There is one circumstance which seems to make this claim of the South, for the further extension of Slave Territory, very unreasonable. The white population of the Slave States is less than one-half that of the Free States: Whilst the territory embraced in the Slave States is more than double that of the Free

States; that is to say, the proportion of land to each individual is four times greater in the Slave than in the Free States. There is no ground, therefore, for saying, on the part of the South, that they are cramped and short of room for expansion.

"So far as I can look on the matter, I cannot see in the Wilmot Proviso the dishonor or oppression to the South which so much excites them. Neither can I see in it any such boon or good to the North which should make them willing for it to disturb the peace of the Union.

"Is this glorious Union to be shaken by mere apprehension of evil? The excitement of the South, showing itself in concerted action, gives me great alarm. It looks to me as if there were ruling spirits who look to disunion as a good; as likely to afford more security to slave property than exists under the present government. It is, I think, a great mistake. I have little fear of an actual dismemberment of the Union. There are difficulties about a peaceable separation which will, I think, be found insuperable. But collision, and even bloodshed, are very ready to happen under such excitement, as seems now to be lashing itself up for action. What might follow such a collision, no mortal can foresee. It is, I think, the duty of every good citizen to do all in his power to prevent any such catastrophe, and to adopt for his motto, 'The Union must be preserved.' I have extended this letter further than I had any idea of doing when I began it. You will agree with me, I am sure, in attachment to the Union, and I trust in the sentiment with which I subscribe myself, very sincerely, your friend."

Whether my reasoning was right or wrong, my apprehensions were but too well founded. The excitement on the Slavery question rapidly increased; when, through the exertions of Mr. Clay and Mr. Webster, in 1850, what was called the Compromise was carried through Congress, affording additional security for the return of fugitive slaves, and admitting California as a Free State. This Compromise seemed to promise an end to the Slavery agitation. There were discontented spirits, but the masses in Massachusetts and New England, and apparently through all the Free States, were satisfied and content—in a state of perfect repose. The South also appeared content, with the exception of South Carolina.

In an evil hour this happy state of things was disturbed by the repeal of the Missouri Compromise, and the introduction of the Kansas Nebraska Bill into Congress, in support of which a majority of the Southern Whigs were induced to join. It was a fatal measure. It roused and alarmed the whole North. It annihilated the great conservative Whig Party, whilst it weakened and crippled the Democratic Party of the North. The Free Soil Party, under the new name of Republican, was recruited and improved by conservative men of both parties, but not in sufficient numbers to control their measures. On the contrary, it enabled the Abolitionists proper to renew their denunciations of Slavery in the abstract, and to call together listening crowds of ultra philanthropists. It is not surprising that in this state of excitement, some legislative measures were adopted which cannot be justified under the Constitution, but will yield to a sober second thought, because they are not the result of any disloyalty to the Union and the Constitution, but the natural reaction of what was considered a Southern aggression.

As the last incident, a man of some character, but of a disordered intellect, John Brown, attempts to excite a slave insurrection in Virginia. He was guilty of treason and murder, for which he justly suffered the penalty of the law. Some rabid Abolitionists and fanatical philanthropists undertook, even in Boston, to glorify him as a martyr. Sober men witnessed this exhibition of folly with silent contempt and disgust, until they found that this silence was, in the South, construed into approval. They then called the meeting in Faneuil Hall, which showed the real feeling of the community, sound, and strong for the Union and the Constitution.

In the meantime, the cry of disunion and secession is raised in certain States of the South. South Carolina sends a distinguished ambassador to your State of Virginia, in order to induce her to send delegates to a Southern Convention, probably thinking the excitement growing out of the attempt at Harper's Ferry presented an opportunity favorable to the adoption of her favorite measure.

The first idea of secession from the Union was started by South Carolina, in 1831. The pretext was the Tariff of 1828. This was called the bill of abominations, and was in some sense rightly named, inasmuch as its opponents adopted the dangerous expedient of making it as bad as possible, in the hopes of thereby defeating it. In 1832, a new tariff was to be made in order to reduce the revenue, after the payment of the national debt. After a long and full discussion, the Tariff of 1832 was passed by an unprecedented majority—132 to 65 in the House of Representatives; about one-half of the majority consisting of the Democratic Party, including the names of James K. Polk, Cave Johnson, G. C. Verplank, C. C. Cambreling, &c. This bill was framed on the principle of raising the necessary revenue, by adjusting the duties on imports, with a view to afford protection to our domestic industry. But this did not suit South Carolina. She had already put herself in the attitude of armed resistance to the revenue laws of the United States. Mr. McDuffie had persuaded her to adopt the theory of which he claimed to be the discoverer, that a duty laid nominally on imports was in fact really a tax upon the exports of a country; and inasmuch as the South furnished most of the exports of the United States, the great burden of the tax fell upon them. He was allowed to embody this theory in an elaborate report of the Committee of Ways and Means, accompanied by a bill reducing all duties to a horizontal level of 12½ per cent. He rested his claim for the South solely on the truth of his new theory, admitting expressly that if the tax fell upon the consumers of the commodities imported, the South had no ground of complaint. It was under these circumstances that South Carolina was prepared to leave the Union by force, in 1832, when General Jackson, in November, issued his famous proclamation, preparing to meet force by force. This was a staggerer. However, on the meeting of the 22d Congress, at their second session, General Jackson, in his Message, took ground against the Tariff of 1832 and the protective system. The ground assigned was that it would produce too much revenue, more than was proposed in a bill prepared by Mr. McLane, Secretary of the Treasury. This, in fact, was not true, as was proved in a Document, (47, 2d sess. 22d Congress). But the mere dictum of General Jackson was sufficient to induce the whole of the Democratic Party to eat their own words of the previous session, and sustain Mr. Verplank's anti-protective bill; but without success. After a violent struggle, that bill was abandoned, and Mr. Clay's Compromise accepted and adopted. This was postponing the evil day until 1841–42. South Carolina claimed it as a victory, and justly, and also postponed her military preparations. I was a member of this 22d Congress, and came to the deliberate conclusion, that whilst South Carolina put forward her view of the Tariff as the ground of complaint, her real object was separation, for separation sake, and the formation of a Southern Confederacy, of which Charleston would be the metropolitan city. This opinion I still entertain, and find it has been adopted and held by those best qualified to form a correct opinion in the matter. The leading motive no doubt was the belief that slave property would be safer from aggression—not unmingled with something of personal ambition. This desire for secession and separation has evidently continued her leading object to the present day. This is the key to her various demonstrations, especially to Virginia, to which you allude. Without Virginia she can do nothing. Virginia stands as the great bulwark of the Union—the keystone of our national arch. This idea of a Southern Confederacy has evidently made some converts in Georgia, Alabama, and Mississippi.

I have thus endeavored to give a fair view of the course of events which have brought about the present unhappy state of feeling. I now proceed to present some views of a practical common-sense character, which appear to me to commend themselves as standing on a basis which cannot be shaken. I say to the North, to the Free States, why agitate or discuss at all the question of Slavery? There are four millions of negro slaves in certain States of the Union, with about seven millions of whites. Between the two races there is an impassable gulf which makes amalgamation or absorption impossible. So strong is this antagonism of race, that many of the Free States pass the most stringent laws, in order to keep free negroes out of their borders, considering them a public nuisance. No sane man can possibly believe that these eleven millions can live together with equal rights, under our institutions. As to emigration, that is equally out of the question. It is utterly inadequate, if desirable. It is not easy to point out where they would be better off. It is doubtful if it would be in any of the West

India Islands, under their new system of Coolies. Certainly not in Canada, where they are not wanted, and where they are miserable. Then there is the question of property, to an amount of thousands of millions of dollars. This to be sure is nothing to a thorough-going Abolitionist, who scouts the idea of making man a chattel. The political economist however, knows that all property is the creature of legislation. Any thing is property which the law makes so. Slaves are therefore property in the Slave States, and we of the Free States have nothing to do with the question. Can any man of common-sense suppose such an amount of property can be abandoned, or annihilated? Slavery has died out when slaves cease to have value, and not before. Where there has been unity of race, they have been absorbed, but with us that is impossible. All attempts of the North therefore, to affect the state of Slavery in the South, are utterly idle and futile. Doubtless some improvement may be made in the treatment of slaves; but this had best be left to the parties interested. All pressure from without is hateful and unjustifiable.

To the South I would say, why continue this useless agitation upon mere abstractions? you have possession of all the territory in which slave labor can be profitably employed, and large enough to allow its expansion for many generations. Why trouble yourselves about slavery in the territories to which it is not suited? Why claim or expect an equality of political power sectionally, when your white population is less than half that of the Free States, with the proportion constantly increasing by foreign emigration? Why threaten disunion unless you can control the presidential election? Your true palladium is the Constitution of the United States. This is your ark of safety. On full and calm consideration, the united North will feel as little inclination as they have power to trouble themselves with your Institution. Why talk of disunion? A peaceable separation is impossible. No sane man can think it otherwise. A Southern Confederacy must of necessity be confined to the territory east of the Mississippi. The great West will never consent to give up the possession of that river as their highway, nor New Orleans as their great market. Who will consent to be the border States, where a new set of abolitionists may set up the business of enticing runaways or exciting insurrection, without remedy? A civil war, or a servile war, may be easily brought about, under excited passions; but a peaceable division of this glorious Union, a voluntary disruption of a great nation, appears to me utterly impossible; as impossible as is the abolition of Slavery. If I am right in my conclusions, there is in reality nothing between the North and the South to quarrel about. The idea that there is an irrepressible conflict between the Free States and the Slave States, is simply absurd and untrue. There is no antagonism between slave labor and free labor, as respects the States. If there is any such antagonism at all, it can only be in those States where the two systems prevail together. This can be no cause for ill blood in the North. If this state of things exist in the South, it would furnish a good argument why they should join the North in wishing for protection to our own industry, in order to bring their white labor into action. The actual condition of the North and the South, in their natural productions, is most favorable to a trade and intercourse mutually advantageous and agreeable. The present estrangement, on the abstract question, is as unnatural as it is unchristian. That mutual interest and mutual good-will may resume their natural functions throughout the nation, is the sentiment with which I subscribe myself, with great regard,

Your friend and very ob't serv't,

NATHAN APPLETON.

Boston, 12th March, 1860.

Hon. Wm. C. Rives.

www.ingramcontent.com/pod-product-compliance
Lightning Source LLC
LaVergne TN
LVHW020637110826
845149LV00004B/1244

* 9 7 8 1 4 1 8 1 9 0 6 7 5 *